the Cellarium Primer

A RULE AND REGIMEN
for the
BROWN SCAPULAR CONFRATERNITY
of
OUR LADY OF MOUNT CARMEL

CONTENTS

DEDICATION

For Our Lady of Mount Carmel

PREFACE

The sky was beginning to darken on the evening on the 16th of August, 2018. My heart was heavy and my body was still in shock after reading through some of the documents released by the grand jury investigation of the Pennsylvania Catholic dioceses. It was merely days before that we learned of now ex-Cardinal Theodore McCarrick's long history of pederasty as he climbed to the Catholic Church's highest ranks amid deafening silence from his brother bishops.

Clearly, the Church is undergoing a purification. Judgment begins in the house of God (1 Peter 4:17). But how should Catholics-in-the-pew react? These symptoms of a larger problem might have some remedy in the actions of policemen and courtrooms, but at a time when it seems that nothing of substance is being done at the highest levels of the hierarchy, I do not believe that the secular powers fall outside of God's plan.

The world, as Chesterton noted, seems to have flipped upside down. Feel free to disagree, but my hunch is that we have nothing to fear from the exposure of clerical crimes and cover ups. We should welcome it. Victory lies on the other side if we embrace God's will for us.

In discussing these woeful topics recently, an acquaintance said that the devil always overplays his hand. I liken it to a careless bike mechanic putting too much air into an inner tube. Eventually the compressed air will discover a weakness in the tube and split the tire. So much, we can hope and pray, for these diabolical plans.

I have recently read with sorrow a number of "farewells" on Catholic social media platforms – justifications for why some people are cutting their ties with the Catholic Church – from those abandoning the ship and swimming for alien spiritual shores. My heart aches for them, because so many of them were abused, or knew someone who was abused, or otherwise waited for justice only to find silence and even direct attack from those who are supposed to be our fathers and shepherds.

I hope that they find their way back home, because now is not the time to abandon the Church. Now is the time to inoculate ourselves against what is still to come, because we are still in the early days of what is going to be a lengthy and painful process. It is time to double down, pleading God with all humility, "make me a Saint."

That is why I put this little book together, in the hope that it will rouse a host of Catholics who desire to get so close to Christ that they can feel his breath on their cheek. I hope that, in these pages, they can discover an answer to the tepidity born of the culture into which we have so thoroughly assimilated.

This is a book to help you pray more, to be formed by that prayer, and to grow strong in virtue, especially the virtues of faith, hope, and the love of God. The way presented here is not easy, but it is necessary.

I have no resume or saintly credentials to offer you. You may have none to offer me. Truth be told, I'm probably the last person on earth who should be writing this book. Historically I have been a lax father, an inconsistent Catholic, a servant who buried his talents in the ground, an habitual sinner who knew better but couldn't find the strength to do much beyond shifting from forgiveness to condemnation to forgiveness like a car passing through patches of sunlight and shadows.

But God will be the agent who contrasts the darkness of our previous lives with the clear light of sanctity. It is He who wills to pour his grace into us so that His name might be glorified and that we might dwell with him in eternal bliss. even beginnin here on earth.

Preface

What are we but dust? *Dust beloved by God for reasons that escape me.* You and I have done nothing to deserve this all-encompassing love, and yet there He hangs, nailed and bloody upon a cross of punishment that we deserved. Why he desires our companionship I dare not question. What I will say is the only ones who will survive what is coming are those with the firm desire to become holy, a real desire to comfort the One who was pierced for our iniquities, and to live authentic Catholic lives *in this troubled age* that honors the blood He shed for us, and to live in a way worthy of that sacrifice.

INTRODUCTION

Cellarium is an apostolate devoted to the formation of those who aspire to sainthood. Being conformed to the universal demands of the Gospel by this method is not an endeavor to be entered into lightly, but I believe it can help guide you to sanctity if you let it. The process begins with the lightest touches of obligation, allowing you to progress in small steps as you begin to implement **a rule of life** and **a daily regimen** based on enrollment in the Brown Scapular Confraternity of Our Lady of Mount Carmel and the spiritual benefits it affords.

Let me state from the outset that those who follow the Cellarium rule and regimen are not by such practices third order Carmelites. Let me also state that it is possible by enrollment into the Brown Scapular Confraternity alone to develop a thoroughly Carmelite spirituality. Even those who without enrollment choose to wear the brown scapular and follow this rule and regimen will share to some extent in such blessings through their efforts to conform their lives to deep prayer and Gospel living.

From the day our Blessed Mother gave the brown scapular to the Carmelite community to the day she appeared at Fatima as Our Lady of Mount Carmel with that same brown scapular dangling from her hand, the world has changed profoundly, but our call to holiness has not. If you are struggling for a foothold in your spiritual life, you'll find solid purchase by gradually implementing the rule and regimen presented here, recorded in a simple daily journal in the pages that follow.

But what is the brown scapular, and why should you wear it? Why do I mention it first? This humble swatch of wool, an abbreviated form of the Carmelite habit, has been described as a sign of salvation, a protection in danger, and a pledge of peace with which we have been asked by Our Lady clothe ourselves. Pious legend has suggested that one day, through the Rosary and the Scapular, Mary will save the world.

If we are to redeem the days that are coming, I am convinced that we must wear the brown scapular at the bidding of Our Lady, pray the Rosary with the fervor of a St. Dominic, and do penance with the austerity of a St. Francis. And we must not hold ourselves at a distance from the Sacred Heart of Jesus or the Sorrowful and Immaculate Heart of Mary. It's time to put our priorities in order.

It has been said that Our Lady desired a confraternity joined to the order originally established around that holy mountain that towers above the plain where Elijah defeated the prophets of Ba'al. This happened after the order was moved to Europe. The heights of holiness reached by so many Carmelite saints are attainable by each of us. Simple laymen and women who take up the cloth of Carmel and strive to live its charisms in their daily lives are as dear to Our Lady of Mount Carmel as her priests and religious, her cloistered prayer warriors and those in active service for the Church around the world.. Through the brown scapular, we all can share in the graces of those holy contemplatives, for we are called to the same contemplation.

What does Cellarium mean?

The name Cellarium, Latin for "The Cellar" is a term from the Middle Ages, and cellarers were those appointed in monasteries and castles to oversee the community's provisions. For those who follow this rule and regimen, there is a double meaning. Cellarium also refers to descending daily into the wine cellar of Christ's love, which is the heart of this apostolate, because it is the one necessary thing, the *"unum necessarium"* that animates the Catholic life.

"He brought me into the cellar of wine, he set in order charity in me; eat, O friends, and drink and be inebriated, my dearly beloved."

- Song of Songs 2:4, 5:1

I do not envision Cellarium requiring anything beyond oneself, family, and local parish community to survive and grow. It will grow in the hearts and minds of those heroic enough to implement it. It is an individual decision that will gain strength through coming together regularly with others who have adopted the same spiritual practices, promoting personal holiness and strengthening the bonds of love.

Putting together these materials and making them available to you is part of my apostolate, but I am not the founder or director of any religious movement, Carmelite or otherwise. The predecessor of this planner was a simple folded sheet of paper with spaces for recording the same information contained in the following pages. It was for myself and for my own progress in holiness. I see this rule and regimen, and the planners based on it as nothing but a slightly more advanced version of something akin to St. Thérèse's sacrifice beads. If used without spiritual pride, it will allow you to prudently record and plan, one week at a time, specifically how you plan to advance in sanctity. If you put the plan into action, you will begin to grow in holiness. It is that simple.

If enough of you find it effective and it gains a following, you will find others formed by the same charism and use it for the good of the Church in your home, parish, community, and workplace. Nothing contained here is a novelty in the history of the Church, I'm simply presenting it in a hopefully understandable and actionable way. It's all about putting on the new man in Christ and living a Gospel lifestyle. That means turning away from sin and back to our loving and merciful God.

Sin decreases where prayer increases, and deeper prayer is rewarded with deeper divine intimacy. If we take our eternal destination seriously, everything that gets in the way of our progress toward sanctity must fall by the wayside. You will find out how to pursue this path each day in concrete ways if you keep reading and use the planner as an aid.

As the laity, we are to practice these tasks in our homes, in the stability of community, and in society at large. What we are to believe, what we are to pray, what mortifications we offer to God in our own bodies, these are things that we owe to God.

I am convinced that living this simple way of the brown scapular confraternity everyday in our homes, workplaces, and parishes, performing little acts of love incubated in deep prayer and self-denial will bear much fruit, both personally and in the world. The Cellarium rule and regimen is one a way to do that.

Before any action, there must be prayer, and the magnitude of the world situation requires that this prayer be deep. It must increasingly trend toward contemplation, in fact contemplation is its goal, which is why we need Carmel as our guide. Our Lord craves no less.

If Cellarium helps a few people to make more time for God in their life each day and to try to live an authentic Gospel lifestyle like I am trying to do, I'll be happy. Sanctity doesn't happen overnight, but if you take the steps recommended here in good faith, you will progress.

The rule and regimen presented in this book are not meant to be implemented in a day or a week. It is the work of a lifetime. Once you begin to dig in, you'll see that. We are creatures of habit, they must be implemented over time, and daily planners are all about the intelligent use of time. A rule and regimen must be livable, or people will quickly abandon it as onerous without making much progress, so be careful not to over-do it as you begin.

Just as one doesn't begin lifting weights with a 300-pound barbell, one doesn't begin to deepen his or her spiritual life by overwhelming their schedule with prayers and penances.

To keep it simple, think of the rule of life as "The Regs" as in regulating your habits in conformity to authentic Gospel living, and the daily regimen as "The Pegs" on which you'll hang those prayers and devotion that are of necessity a daily occurance. Doing so will begin to form your character, countering those selfish inclinations that say, "my time is mine, I will do with it as I please."

Introduction

In the two section that follow, I'll explain The Regs, and then the Pegs. After that will follow a section that explains in graphic detail, step by step how to determine where you'll begin in each category and actually begin using the planner. From my own experience, though like you I still have a long way to go, Cellarium will assist you in planning intelligently a sure route to holiness. I'm also seasoned enough to know that the best plans can quickly get shredded by reality, which is why it is scalable on a weekly basis, so you don't lose heart or feel like you're returning to square one. You won't be. You'll be returning only to the last sure foothold.

My purpose in writing this book was to offer an aid to those who want to become Saints, myself included. But I would be remiss if I didn't give you a taste of what might lay ahead of you should you pursue this with all your being.

There are few accounts of how one progresses from "glory to glory" through the early stages of prayer and to infused contemplation apart from St. Teresa of Avila's explanation using the metaphor she calls the seven mansions. What follows is adapted from Fr. Thomas Dubay, S.M.'s book "Fire Within" pages 80-107.

In the first three mansions, the Saint says little about prayer. This is because the first stages of prayer (in the first three mansions) depend mostly on the state of our soul (we must be in a state of grace) an our willingness to conform ourselves to the demands Christ makes of us in the Gospels. She likens this prayer to drawing water from a well. where in the final four mansions, prayer is more and more infused and does not depend on our efforts. She likens such prayer to rain, which we do not cause to fall or to stop falling.

What she was adamant about is that prayer while occupying these mansions is a matter of love over form. When we are in love, we want to please the one we love, and avoid doing those things which displease. Attitude (love), posture (respect), and gesture (communion) all have their parts to play, which is why the Church has always decked her public liturgies with fine details. But progress in holiness, and moving deeper into the mansions, has it's own prerequisites.

First mansions - Get rid of sins, imperfections, and earthly attachments. Keep yourself in a state of grace and strive to rid yourself of petty faults and leave the spirit of the world behind. All prayer should be a matter of love, not of method or reasoning. It is the love that is important, along with the practice of praising God at all times and thanking Him with deep gratitude and thanksgiving in all things.[1]

Second mansions - While everything in the first mansions continues into the second, you will begin to sense a tug-of-war between the world and earthly pleasures and God's call. You will feel called to acts of self-denial but often avoid them out of weakness. There is a growing conviction to press on toward God and leave earthly pleasures behind. You will desire to gain deeper humility, obedience, love and patience, but will still be a baby in their practice. You will find that your prayer life will not deepen until you begin to deepen your commitment to Gospel living. During this time, it is important to avoid close association with evil. Avoid spending time with the spiritually mediocre and seek the fellowship of those who are more spiritually advanced than you. Embrace suffering for and with Christ generously; welcome hardships and dryness in prayer. Resolve to conform yourself to God's will in all things. When you fall (and you will), get up, dust yourself off, and continue walking.

Third mansions - In the third mansions, the conscience is becoming more tender. You will avoid even venial sins and the thought of doing penances and practicing self-denial is no longer fearsome to you, rather the fear turns into love. You will find yourself more and more in a recollected state and will have begun to use your time well. Practicing the corporal and spiritual works of mercy will become more frequent. Modesty in dress as well as keeping diligent watch over your tongue will noticibly intensify. There will be an increased attention toward always doing God's will.

In general terms, one has little need of spiritual direction in the first three mansions. That changes abruptly in the fourth.

Fourth mansions - St. Teresa says that many souls experience the beginnings of what she calls infused contemplation. In the fourth mansions, the prayer that we attain of our own efforts begins to mix with infused prayer over which we have no con-

---

1   Dubay, "Fire Within" p. 81

trol. There are dangers here because people don't know how to adjust from one to the other. Spiritual direction becomes more of a necessity here.

Initially, most people who advance this far experience it as a deep supernatural recollection, different from our own weak natural recollection. In addition some experience what Teresa calls the prayer of quiet. It can take several forms, but is an imageless, loving awareness of God, often felt as dry desire or a strong thirst. It can be felt as a delicate touch or in later stages a longer, immersive, burning love. As this infused prayer progresses, God binds the will, but the intellect and imagination are left to some degree free to operate.

Fifth mansions - In the fifth mansions, the soul experiences what St. Teresa calls full union with God. In it, the will, intellect, and imagination are held in near total captivity, being occupied completely by God. The distractions experienced in the fourth mansions are gone. The character of this absorption is one of delight. This stage of prayer is further marked by abandonment of self-centeredness, growing as it is in love an an inner freedom to love others with the love of God. These encounters are usually brief but intense.

Sixth mansion - In these mansions one experiences a deepening of the previous immersions. Characteristic of the union are ecstasy, rapture, and transport, along with experiences of the wounds of love, spiritual betrothal, and even levitation. The inner live has so been taken over by God that sense perception for all intent disappears. Such ecstasy and the attendant loss of the senses is very short, but when the intellect and the wil return, they are absorbed again into the will. This fluctuating experience can last for several hours at a time.

Seventh mansions - St. Teresa calls this seventh and final mansion the transforming union. It is a spiritual marriage of the soul to the Triune God. At first, one is enveloped in a cloud of intense brightness and sees the three Persons of the Holy Trinity though not with the eyes. In this encounter, the soul sees Jesus in an intellectual vision just as He appeared to the Apostles after the Resurrection. The oneness with the Lord becomes permanent as a constant and gentle awareness. People who reach the seventh mansion are able to carry on with the ordinary business of their daily lives, and experience near perfection in loving God with all the heart, mind, soul and strength, and in loving others as Christ has loved us. While a person in this permanent state possesses the inner peace and repose of being constantly aware of the Lord's presence, he or she is not freed from suffering from the sins of others, of any of the difficulties of living in this valley of tears, but they experience the permanent inner calm of the complete union of their soul with the Beloved.

This is what I wish for all of us. I wish it for you, and for myself, and for all. I believe that Cellarium has the capacity to help you to get from St. Teresa's third mansion and into the fourth. Maybe I'll be proven wrong, but I'm willing to give it my all. Will you?

In Charity,

Jim

A RULE OF LIFE
"THE REGS"

Let's briefly go over the individual practices included in the Cellarium rule and regimen. It's not to scare you, but to forewarn you that this isn't some vapid set of guidelines to make you feel good about yourself. The elements of Cellarium are:

- To wear the brown scapular day and night
- To observe chastity according to your state in life
- To fast or abstain from meat on Wednesdays and Saturdays, in addition to Friday abstinence.
- To pray the Rosary each day
- To daily pray some part of the Liturgy of the Hours or the Little Office of the Blessed Virgin Mary
- Daily contemplative prayer
- Intercession
- Conspicuous silence
- Gospel poverty
- Daily Mass or reading the Liturgy of the Word
- Spiritual reading, if possible the day's entry from Fr. Gabriel of Saint Mary Magdalene's "Divine Intimacy"
- Keeping the Lord's Day holy by, in addition to attending Sunday Mass, gathering for fellowship with other believers

Again, a reminder that you won't be implementing these all at once, and for some people, it may take months or more to get there. It isn't a race, it's a way of life. Lets go into detail.

THE BROWN SCAPULAR

The brown scapular has been hailed as a sign of salvation, a protection in danger, and a pledge of peace. In modern language, the way that Carmelites today phrase it is that it is a sign of our consecration to Our Lady of Mount Carmel. It is her protective mantle, thrown over our shoulders with maternal care. The brown scapular is the habit of Carmel, whether worn by Carmelite priests or religious, a third order, the confraternity, or even one who has no connection to the order but lives a Carmelite spirituality.

This spirituality is marked by living a life of supernatural grace, chastity, prayer and penance, which has taken several forms over the past 750-plus years. These will be explained in a moment.

In previous times, many of the practices in the Cellarium rule and regimen were closely tied to the requirements for gaining the Sabbatine Privilege, which said that those who wore the scapular, persevered in charity, observed chastity, and recited the Little Office of the Blessed Virgin Mary (or in lieu of the LOBVM observed the fast days of the Church and abstained from flesh meat on Wednesdays and Saturdays) would be released from purgatory on the Saturday after their death.

Even without a sure guarantee that such will be the case, the Church has continued to recommend the brown scapular of Our Lady of Mount Carmel for reasons that extend beyond any historical inaccuracies or pious fables.

Of most recent memory is the fact that during the final apparition of Our Lady of Fatima, she came clothed in the habit of Carmel, and Sister Lucy has stated that "the scapular and the Rosary are inseparable. The scapular is a sign of consecration to Our Lady. [She] wants all to wear the scapular."

Carmelite spirituality lived through the Confraternity does not conflict with other forms of Catholic spirituality. Many, in fact, including St. Don Bosco of the Salesians and St. Alphonsus Ligouri of the Redemptorists were members of the brown scapular Confraternity.

The approved rite for the enrollment in the brown scapular can be found in the final pages of this planner.

CHASTITY

The second part of the Cellarium rule of life concerns sexual purity. Practicing chastity according to one's state in life is simple to explain but often difficult to explain when countering arguments. Essentially, the Church teaches that the marital embrace is reserved to those validly married. There are no exceptions for anyone else. One's state in life is either single, married, or vowed to celibacy. The single believer is bound to chastity out of respect that we were bought at a great price and because our bodies are temples and the Holy Trinity indwells us. Also out of respect for one's future spouse.

The married are called to chastity and to flee even the temptation to adultery. Sacramental marriage is between a man and a woman under a covenant that remains until the death of one of the spouses. Priests and vowed religious are bound to celibacy as long as their vows are intact, and they choose Christ as bridegroom forsaking all others. The Church is the bride of Christ, Christ is the bridegroom, and priests and vowed religious image that truth in their bodies as they allow the pure flower of their virginity to blossom while serving the Church unburdened by the obligations and privileges of marriage.

Modern society suggests to all, even children, that their right to practice all forms of sexual impurity is absolute. The atmosphere is polluted with images and suggestive messages that such impurity is a virtue. And so we are constantly bombarded with the temptation to sin against chastity. St. Paul tells us in 1 Corinthians 6:18 that every other sin we can commit is outside of our body, but those who sin against chastity sin against their own bodies.

But here is a secret that should be more widely known and recommended. Wearing the brown scapular puts you under the protective mantle of our Lady. It offers protection in danger, including against impure thoughts, and when combined with the other elements of the promise, sets one up for success when fighting against impurity.

We can believe with confidence that the protection against danger that Our Lady offers to those who choose to live under the mantle of her scapular is both real and tangible. Those who have been enrolled in the brown scapular and wear it constantly often find that on those occasions where they had to remove it for some reason, even for a short period of time, the enemy attacks in ways he cannot when the believer is wearing it.

THE WINE CELLAR

The driving force behind Cellarium begins in the wine cellar, descending every day into the depth of that good place to, as John Senior quotes from the Canticle of Canticles, "Eat, O my friends, and drink, and be inebriated, my dearly beloved..."

Think of this in terms of the great Carmelite Saints Teresa of Avila and John of the Cross. It is the beginning of a journey toward what these Spanish mystics called the transforming union. It would be folly for me to try to attempt to explain it in depth in a short chapter prefacing a daily planner. But it is important to understand that your experiences up to now regarding prayer will not continue along the same dusty road you may have taken until now. As one's prayer life grows, and as attachment to sin and to creatures weakens in the light of God's love for your soul, there will come a transition. Teresa explained it with two images. Prayer at first is like drawing water from a well. But as natural contemplation is replaced by infused contemplation, your prayer will begin to change. God is attracted to our love and when He sees us beginning to love Him without reserve to the best of our ability, He comes to our aid. Where our prayers were once toilsome like pulling it up from the well, He begins to rain it down upon us without our effort.

You begin the process by taking the time and making the commitment to show up, to descend with Him each day into the wine cellar of His love. There is no replacement for this in the life of a Catholic.

Just as we feign allegiance to Christ when we allow ourselves to remain in habitual mortal sin, as we press toward our life's goal, which is the Beatific Vision, eventually even our venial sins and little imperfections will pain us as we draw closer to the lover of our souls. Sin decreases where prayer increases, and deep prayer is rewarded with deep intimacy.

If we take our eternal destination seriously, everything that gets in the way of our progress toward sanctity must fall by the wayside. You must begin the process by the simple act of scheduling this time into your day and showing up.

When we visit our friends, we usually have something to tell them, or a question to ask. It is not much different with God. For those without a history of praying seriously, it might be unnerving to dwell with Him for a time each day in silence.

There is no need to be worried, however. The Cellarium rule and regimen offers spiritual topics each day for meditation, especially from keeping the Hours, as we'll discuss in more detail in a few moments, the daily Mass readings, or the day's chapter from the book Divine Intimacy.

There is often enough to ponder silently from a single passage from one of these readings to send the soul more deeply into the wine cellar, further from the written words on a page or from a prayer, into meditation upon some aspect of it, deeper into natural contemplation, and as God allows, finally into infused contemplation.

THE ROSARY

If you haven't learned yet how to pray the Rosary, now is the time to begin. The Rosary is on its face a series of simple prayers, accompanied by meditation on some of the key mysteries in the history of our redemption. The strung beads themselves are a sacramental blessed by a priest, and praying it involves the whole person: the hands move over the beads, the mouth recites the prayers, and the mind meditates on the mysteries. But what Mary has revealed to us is that the Rosary is a powerful spiritual weapon. All of the graces and favors we receive from God, we receive through her intercession. There are some graces and favors we can only receive from her intercession with her Son, as is the case with the rest of the Saints.

This is a great mystery in itself, but because of Mary's unique role in salvation history, her perfect cooperation with grace, and the union of her heart with her Son's heart, she has a singular role to play in each of our lives. She is the mother of Christ. We are Christ's brothers, and Mary is also our mother in that sense. Just as Christ gave Mary to "the beloved disciple" John at the foot of the Cross on Calvary, so He gives her to every "beloved disciple."

Mary asks us to pray her Rosary because it is by this means that *we participate with her* in creating graces otherwise unattainable, both for others and for ourselves. By praying the Rosary we participate with her in crushing the head of the ancient serpent.

As I have said, the Rosary is not simply a prayer, not simply a meditation, not simply a moving of the fingers over the beads. It is a spiritual weapon with power beyond our comprehension. Our Lord unleashes unimaginable graces on those who unite their hearts with his Sacred Heart and Mary's Sorrowful and Immaculate Heart.

Why is this? We get a glimpse of it in the Old Testament book of 1 Kings. Consider that as the mother of the heir to David's throne, Mary held a special place in the Davidic kingdom. She is the queen mother. The queen mother's royal duty was to present requests to the king from his subjects.

When Solomon was made king by his father David, his rival Adonijah presented himself before Bathsheba, who had just become the queen mother upon David's death. He has a request for Solomon, and it was her duty to deliver it. Here is what transpired, from the Douay Rheims (with names modernized):

"Then Bathsheba came to king Solomon, to speak to him for Adonijah, and the king arose to meet her, and bowed to her, and sat down upon his throne and a throne was set for the king's mother, and she sat on his right hand.

"And she said to him, 'I desire one small petition of thee, do not put me to confusion.' And the king said to her, 'My mother, ask, for I must not turn away thy face.' - 1 Kings 2:19-20

"For I must not turn away thy face" is another way of saying what Adonijah suggested to her, "for he cannot deny thee any thing."

When we pray the Rosary, we are taking our requests to the King through His Queen Mother whom he gave us also as our mother.

We should always do so for specific intentions. When we do this, we are quite literally placing those people and things into her care. Mary's relationship to the Holy Spirit is not to be discounted. The eternal uncreated Widsom who descended upon her and overshadowed her at the moment of Christ's conception remains with her and there is no knot that the Wisdom of God cannot untie. There is no problem too difficult for Widsom to solve. There is no need so great that Wisdom cannot satisfy. When we pray the Rosary for specific people and intentions, it is as though we are going to Mary, taking her hand and saying, "Mother, come here. Can you help him? Can you fix this?"

Yes, the Rosary is prayer, and a sacramental, but it is also a deadly weapon against the enemies of God and a gift given us by our Mother to foil the plans of the enemy and a means of securing special graces on those for whom we pray. How could we not pray it?

In praying the Rosary we are putting ourselves and our very sanctification in the hands of Our Lady. We are putting a wedge between ourselves and the evil one because he hates Mary and flees from her. God has put enmity between her and the ancient serpent. If we cling to her, he will flee from us. Each day, we should pray at least part of the Rosary.

INTERCESSION

As intercessors for those who ask for our prayers and for those for whom we should be praying even without their requesting it, we should make a prayer list and keep it updated at all times. It should become like breathing for those who take the commandments of Our Lord seriously: Love the Lord your God with all your heart, mind, soul and strength, and your neighbor as yourself. Yes, even as He has loved us.

Praying for others is the chief way we love others as He has loved us. Yes, we also owe them in justice that which is within our means to provide in the way of food and shelter, clothing and comfort. But without intercession we cannot truly be for others, and will revert back into the natural tendency toward self-ishness.

The practice of keeping and using a prayer list will make you a true intercessor, and one of those through whom Christ will work to save souls: Unite your Rosary to your prayer list!

We should always pray the Rosary for certain intentions.

Start your list by relationship and family ties first. This main list does not have to be part of your planner, and I'll explain why in a moment. There is much to be said for placing it in an app that allows you to access it and update it wherever you are.

Your parents, siblings, aunts and uncles and their children, and so on. Include everyone whom you can remember, even groups such as "my friends from parochial school" or "those with whom I served in the military." Once you have written these down, it will be easier to flesh it out later as more names come to mind. If some of these have died, still write their names down, perhaps in a separate section. After your family, add your friends, associates and acquaintances. After these, start adding those who have asked you to pray for them or for someone else. You will find yourself adding to this list frequently. When you do, remember to look over the rest of the list. It may uncover opportunities to follow up with people who have asked you to pray.

This also tells them that you were actually praying for their stated need. There will be times when our Lord brings specific people to mind, people that you then pray for. But by adding these people to your Rosary intentions, you will be praying for them as often as you pray the Rosary.

Of course, if someone asks you in person to pray for them, never hesitate to do so. Something that has always struck me as beautiful about many of our separated brethren is that when someone asks them to pray for them, to do so right then and there. It can be intimidating for some Catholics who are used to, at most, offering an Our Father, Hail Mary, and Glory Be. It doesn't have to be that way.

St. Pio of Pietrelcina was bombarded with specific prayer requests, and those who keep his life history relate that his favorite prayer in such cases, which often resulted in miraculous cures and divine interventions, was the Effecacious Novena to the Sacred Heart of Jesus.

Novenas are not incantations where if one word is said wrong the whole prayer is ineffectual. What matters is that we pray with faith in love. The novena Padre Pio prayed is based on scriptural promises given by Our Lord, asked by us through His Sacred Heart. Here are the petitions which you can quickly commit to memory and use when someone asks you to pray for them:

O my Jesus you have said, "truly I say to you, ask and you will receive, seek and you will find, knock and it will be opened to you." And so Lord I knock, I seek, and I ask that you (say your request), through your Sacred Heart of Jesus, I place all my trust in you.

O my Jesus you have said, "If you ask anything of the Father in my name, he will give it to you." Lord, in your name I ask the Father for (say your request). Sacred Heart of Jesus, I place all my trust in you.

O my Jesus you have said, "Heaven and earth will pass away but my words will not pass away." Lord, I believe you and ask (say your request). Sacred Heart of Jesus, I place all my trust in you.

O Sacred Heart of Jesus, you who have compassion on the afflicted, take pity on us and grant our prayer through the Sorrowful and Immaculate Heart of Mary, Mother of God and our Mother.

The intentions we offer up with our Rosaries will be acted upon. Even if it seems that our prayers are not answered, we have assurance that the grace is applied every single time at someone's point of need. We should have no fear that our prayers go unanswered. Finally, regular recitation of the Rosary will conform our lives to its mysteries. As we share the joys, the sorrows, the glories, and bask in the light of the mysteries, we will advance ever closer to Christ's heart.

The prayer sections in this planner, on the daily, weekly, and quarterly spaces, are designed to reinforce the prayer and intercession. You will find that each daily spread has a section for writiing down the people and things you're asked to pray for, or in any case, those people and things for which you should be praying. At the end of each day, you should take a moment to move those people and things to the weekly Intercessory Prayer pages located right after each Weekly Preview. This gives you an opportunity to bring them to mind again, and the simple act of transferring them over is an opportunity to pray for them again. At the end of the week, you'll repeat the process, but will be moving the Weekly Prayers into the Quarterly Prayers section. If you are also keeping a separate prayer list somewhere (which is a prudent thing to do because quarterly planners have pretty short lives) you can repeat the process four times a year or more often. The point is to continually bring them to mind and pray for them.

CONSPICUOUS SILENCE

"Noise is the twin brother of the lie. Silence is the seat of truth, the dwelling place of God¹."

Professed Carmelites observe a limited silence, normally from bedtime until waking, or from the end of night prayer until morning prayer. But for those of us who live in the world, we should observe that which prudence suggests in our circumstances. We must seek out pools of silence in the landscape of our day. The greatest reason why is that without silence, we cannot be recollected. And without recollection, we can not achieve deep communion with God or approach contemplation. God dwells in silence. If we live in noise, we cannot hear Him.

Elijah had an encounter with the Lord, an encounter that is central to Carmelite spirituality. In 1 Kings 19:11-13, after Elijah had defeated the prophets of Ba'al and had taken shelter in a cave, God told him to stand on the mountain and the Lord would pass by him.

First a mighty wind arose so strong that it crushed rocks. Elijah didn't recognize God in the mighty wind. Next, an earthquake shook the mountain, but God was not in the earthquake. Then fire erupted, but God was not in the fire, either. Finally, Elijah heard the still, small whisper of a voice. When he heard

1   Robert Cardinal Sarah, *The Day is Now Far Spent, 2019 Ignatius Press,* p. 250

this, he pulled up his cloak to hide his face, and stood at the entrance of the cave.

God dwells in sacred silence. We must meet him there. That is why it is important to have a quiet place to go and pray. It's why we need a wine cellar in which to meet the Beloved.

Another important reason why we should practice silence more often is because it is very easy for us to sin with our tongues. When we hear these passages read at Mass or read them for ourselves, we often gloss over them and ignore them. But we do so to our own injury.

Life under the rule and regimen is not a life of complete silence, rather it is a prudent silence. It suggests custody of the tongue.

Jesus tells us in Matthew 12:35-37 that on the day of judgment we will have to give an account for every idle word we ever spoke. He said that a good man brings forth good things from his stores, and an evil man brings forth evil things, and that we will be justified or condemned based not only on our deeds, but on what we have said.

St. Paul in Colossians 3:8-9 tells us that as followers of Christ we must set aside anger, malice, insults, foul language and lies. There are no exceptions

We are not to bicker, complain, gossip, or attack. Our priority is to love. It is not a love that turns a blind eye to injustice but it is a love that sees the logs in our own eyes instead of the speck in our neighbor's. It is a love that prays for instead of judging, because the charism of love is more powerful than the office of correction. In fact, the first three spiritual works of mercy belong in a particular way to the ordained: to counsel the doubtful, instruct the ignorant, and admonish the sinner. Even in those rare instances where we must practice these works such as within our homes, it should always be done with love, and by humbly assuming that we are a greater sinner than the one we are correcting. And it is love rather than correction that draws our hearts to His Sacred Heart.

GOSPEL POVERTY

The materialistic world we live in, with its keen focus on consumption of superfluous goods, promotes the love of things over the love of God and neighbor. We know in our hearts that this is wrong. Popes and Saints have told us it is wrong. It is directly opposed to the type of life the Gospel demands of a disciple of Jesus Christ.

These are difficult words, yes, but the reality for a Catholic is that we are stewards of that which God has allowed us to accumulate, and beyond our necessities, we sin greatly in not distributing *from what we have* to the poor. If this sounds like insanity, know that it is mandated by Our Lord, and is the very definition of justice: Giving to others from our possessions what we owe them. What do we owe them? St. John the Baptist answered this question succinctly: Whoever has two coats should share with the one who has none, and whoever has food shoud do the same.

It is easier for a camel to pass through the eye of a needle than for a rich man to enter into the kingdom of God. -Mark 10:25

In the parable of Lazarus and the Rich Man in Luke 16:19-31, the rich man who ignored the beggar at his gate was cast into hell, having received his comfort in this world.

No one can serve two masters. For either he will hate the one, and love the other: or he will sustain the one, and despise the other. You cannot serve God and mammon. -Matthew 6:24

And that [seed] which fell among thorns, are they who have heard, and going their way, are choked with the cares and riches and pleasures of this life, and yield no fruit. -Luke 8:14

So likewise every one of you that doth not renounce all that he possesseth, cannot be my disciple. - Luke 14:33

And if a brother or sister be naked, and want daily food: And one of you say to them: Go in peace, be ye warmed and filled; yet give them not those things that are necessary for the body, what shall it profit? - James 2: 15-16

He that hath the substance of this world, and shall see his brother in need, and shall shut up his bowels from him: how doth the charity of God abide in him? My litttle children, let us not love in word, nor in tongue, but in deed, and in truth. - 1 John 3:17-18

And he said to all: If any man will come after me, let him deny himself, and take up his cross daily, and follow me. -Luke 9:23

Finally, in what might be the most dreadful day in the history of the human race, we read that at the last judgment, our eternal fate will rest on how we treated the least:

"Depart from me, you cursed, into everlasting fire which was prepared for the devil and his angels. For I was hungry and you gave me not to eat: I was thirsty, and you gave me not to drink. I was a stranger, and you took me not in: naked, and you covered me not: sick and in prison, and you did not visit me."

We are to find our happiness in the love of God and our neighbor, and this can be broken down simply in the great commandment and the new commandment: Love God with all our heart, mind, soul, and strength and love others as Our Lord has loved us. In doing so, we can become wholly love, but only when we love God totally, and love others with His love.

Can we overlook the words of Christ and the Apostles and find any justification in our unjust actions? Fr. Thomas Dubay, writing in "Happy Are You Poor" reminds us that our destiny is heaven, and nothing on this earth can equal advanced possession of God through immersion in contemplative prayer. He says we can only understand the New Testament teaching on our use of material goods in this light. We can only love God to the extent we are freed from the desire for anything less than God.

Yet if we fail to fulfill the demands of justice, it is impossible to have a deep experience of God.

Self-indulgence and excess is so foreign to the gospel, but living in luxury, pampering ourselves with comforts and numbing ourselves against the harsh realities of the world is an absurdity mostly hidden from our eyes because of the unhinged consumerism of the throwaway society that envelops us.

The truth is that our commitment must be one-hundred percent or it is nothing and will count as nothing.

We are foreigners in this world, on pilgrimage to our forever home, and we must view others as our fellow travelers, sharing with them those things which will help them to their destination, not hinder them.

Being poor with the poor Christ entails an emptiness that assumes the readiness to live here and now as subjects of the Kingdom. When we empty ourselves of any claim on possessions, we stand in expectation of being filled utterly with God. One who has emptied himself for the Lord is open to anything that the Gospel requires. Dubay likens it to a shift in our center of gravity, from ourselves to the bosom of the Holy Trinity.

Concretely, solidarity with suffering mankind in poorer nations and even within our own borders and communities demands that we treat the poor as our brothers and sisters, and provide them food, clothing and shelter at the very least. We must spare of ourselves and share what is left with others. We do not fulfill our obligation to perform the corporal and spiritual works of mercy solely by stuffing a few bills into the collection plate. If we see our brother in need and say to him "be well" without giving him the necessities that wellness requires, *we are going to hell* unless we repent and change our ways. Christ did not mince words on the matter, he said "depart from me."

If we don't adopt the radical poverty that the Gospel demands, we are fakes, and the world can see it on display because nothing distinguishes us from them. Our manner of living reveals what we believe. The good life is not economic for the authentic Catholic, it is justice toward God and others. Holy poverty is also prophetic, because it operationalizes the commands of Christ in the New Testament.

The life of a disciple is ascetic. But what it demands of us, the narrow gate, carrying our cross and dying with our Lord, renouncing all possessions, is replaced with the infinitely finer, the true, the good, the beautiful, and over all that unspeakable joy of being immersed in love the blazing fire of God's love. even here on earth.

In practical terms the minimum requirements, those which apply to everyone, are that we view our possessions through the filter of whether or not they will help us reach heaven, to share our wealth and possessions to the point of rough equality with the poor, to have and use only what we need, and to get rid of what we don't.

Having more than we need dulls our yearning for God and

our desire for prayer. Making spiritual poverty a reality in our lives will mark us as a prophetic witnesses.

FASTING AND FEASTING

Abstinence is a form of fasting. Fasting and self-denial are not personal preferences that can be discarded if we find them difficult. Fasting also gives us spiritual authority. Jesus explained in Matthew 17:21 that certain types of evil spirits can only be driven out through prayer and fasting. When we are fasting, we shouldn't put on a sour face or parade around acting pious. It is a hidden thing.

Cellarium recommends that we abstain from meat with the Church on Fridays, and fast or abstain on Wednesdays and Saturdays. Abstaining from meat is a type of fasting, but fasting itself is only required of a Catholic by the Church two days per year: on Ash Wednesday and Good Friday. This applies to those between the ages of 18 to 59.

Every Catholic over the age of 14 should abstain from meat on Fridays; during Lent, this is under pain of sin. Many today present skillfully crafted arguments why they don't have to abstain. "The Church no longer requires it" they say. "We can substitute some other form of mortification or do something nice for someone instead." But the Church didn't abolish Friday abstinence, she decreed that it is no longer a sin not to do so. The reason the Church removed the penalty of sin is so that *our freely willed mortification would be more efficacious*: so that it would produce more grace. Quite the opposite occurred. Hardly a Catholic abstains from meat on Fridays outside of Lent anymore, nor do they acquire the spiritual authority over fallen angels that self-denial affords.

If Sunday is a mini-Easter, then Friday is a mini-Lent. It should be so for us. Besides, those who produce counter-arguments to the practice, as one might suspect, often fail to implement the alternatives they suggest. Why not just abstain from meat? The answer might be simple. It is because we are unaccustomed to applying any such self-regulation. We want to be free to do what we wish, always.

But choosing some other mortification or doing something nice for someone, whatever that means, fails to produce a necessary reality in the Christian life: Spiritual influence. Fasting creates it, not wearing a penny in your shoe or buying your kid an ice cream cone.

Taking it to the next level might entail fasting on one of those three days instead of just abstaining from meat. According to the Church, fasting consists of eating one full meal, and the other two meals together should not equal one regular meal. But that is the bare minimum. To increase the austerity of the practice as one becomes accustomed to it, one might eat only the one meal, or partake of only bread and water. Or beer. Seriously, beer is okay unless you're disposed toward alcoholism. Monks used to fast on beer, calling it "liquid bread." Just don't drink to excess. There are many people nowadays who are resorting to extreme fasting for its recently discovered health benefits, and they're doing it for secular reasons. Cannot we, who are doing it for faith reasons, match their intensity?

DAILY MASS OR MASS READINGS

Your individual circumstances, state in life and local availability will determine whether or not you are able to find space in your day to attend daily Mass even periodically. But the daily Mass readings are within easy reach of anyone willing to take the time to meditate on them.

If there is one thing that can easily unite us to the Church, her seasons, her calendar full of solemnities, feasts, and memorials and to her very mind on a daily basis, it is the smorgasbord of prayers and readings from the Holy Sacrifice of the Mass.

It might be difficult for some busy people to fit in even one daily Mass per month, but the readings are always available, and no Catholic should let a day pass by without partaking of at least part of the banquet. When we cannot attend the Eucharistic feast, we can make a spiritual Communion. Likewise, when we cannot attend the Liturgy of the Word, the words are still at our disposal.

The readings can really set the tone for the day and allow us to delve deeper into the mysteries of our Faith if we let them wash over us and form us. By this practice, we are immediately made familiar with the Saint of the day (when there is a feast or memorial), and are swept along day by day through the Psalms, the Epistles, and the words of Our Lord in the Gospel.

In addition, there is always much to ponder from the Introit (think "intro") and the Collect. Many parishes have returned to using the Introit at daily Mass since there are rarely hymns as there are at Sunday Mass. "Gathering Hymns" long ago supplanted the Introit at Sunday Mass, which had previously been chanted as priests and servers approached the altar in the Extraordinary Form of Mass. The Collect is the prayer the priest says at the end of the introductory rites, after he goes to the chair and says, "let us pray." Many of these Collects are almost as ancient as the Church, and the most recent revision to the Mass texts have restored much of their beauty and complexity of thought that had been stripped away for a time.

All of these texts pull us into the story of our own redemption as sons and daughters of the Church. They truly do imbue us with the mind of the Church. There is enough meat, as St. Paul would say, to satisfy the hungriest heart. They are ripe for meditation and contemplation through the practice of Lectio Divina, which means divine reading and consists of slowly and carefully reading the words with a prayerful attitude, letting whatever touches you deeply be absorbed into your soul, spending time contemplating it in the presence of God, and then striving to live it.

The daily readings are available online from the USCCB website or you can subscribe to have them delivered to yoru email inbox each day. The site and service do not include the Introit or the Collect.

For those who go into it for the long haul, there are durable daily and Sunday Missalettes available from Catholic Book Publishing Company and such, but many find it easier to subscribe to monthly missalette providers such as Magnificat, Give Us This Day, Word Among Us, and the like. Not that it will interest you much but I prefer the WAU digital subscription for iPhone.

SPIRITUAL FORMATION

One of the things some might consider suspect in an apostolate promoting a rule and regimen based on Carmelite spirituality is the lack of formation that comes from being a religious or third order member. The fact has not gone unnoticed by some within the Carmel family. To put it benignly, there is more than one opinion on whether the Church's decision to allow any priest to enroll members into the Confraternity was a good thing.

Historically, confraternities (not just Carmel) were associations of laypersons who met together regularly and received at least some level of formation. In forming this apostolate and these materials over the past several months, this has not escaped my attention, and I would be remiss if I said that it does not present some problems. But I think these problems can be overcome.

Some rue the fact that people are and have for some time been indiscriminately enrolled in the brown scapular, that it was once widely done at a child's First Holy Communion, that no records were required to be kept, and that what has become more the *idea* of a Confraternity was becoming more and more historically removed from its roots. Fr. Sam anthony Morello, OCD states in a scapular catechesis[2] that ideally, "Confraternity members would have met regularly, participated in devotions together, and had a sense of identity with one another and identification with the Order."

"In the end, when all is said and done, the scapular is the Carmelite habit. Carmelite tradition declares...that the Carmelites enjoy a special protection by the Mother of God as a sign of her love for us and her appreciation of our trust and confidence in her and our devotion to her as our model for living a life of allegiance to her Son.

"We Carmelites are willing even anxious to share this protection and favor that Mary shows us as we are anxious to share the trust and confidence we place in her and our devotion to her. A

---

2   meditationsfromcarmel.com/content/scapular-catechesis

visible sign of our sharing this protection and this devotion is the scapular.

"The Carmelite Order in both its observances should seriously look at reviving the Scapular Confraternity and reorganizing it in actual chapters under the guidance of the Carmelite family to spread an authentic devotion to the Mother of God as it is expressed in our Carmelite tradition.

"To this end, the Order should seek to revoke permission for any but Carmelite Religious to enroll the faithful in the Confraternity and enroll only those who are committed to actual and active membership in a confraternity."

I think that such a reinvigoration of the Confraternity would be a blessing to the entire Catholic Church. Confraternity members most certainly should be formed in the thought and charisms of the Order and it's Saints. As the rite of enrollment states, they *participate in all the spiritual benefits of the Order of Carmel.* Should they not be formed in the charisms that produce those spiritual benefits?

While Fr. Morello is rightly concerned about the external regulation and care of the Confraternity, we do not know the full extent of the internal graces and benefits made available to so many of the faithful by their enrollment in the Confraternity with or without formation.

I can only attest to how my own formation is changing my life, and recommend to you the source.

It is a book called **Divine Intimacy,** written by Father Gabriel of St. Mary Magdalene, OCD, and is a collection of daily meditations on the interior life for each day of the year. Each day's meditation is broken into four parts. It begins with placing oneself in the presence of God and reciting short prayer. This is followed by two meditations and a "colloquy" or conversation with God, usually taken from the writings of Carmelite Saints. When read in a recollected state, Divine Intimacy is a sure path by which to climb Mount Carmel and unearth the treasures hidden there.

A minor flaw, which is not insurmountable, is that the book was written before the liturgical changes of Vatican II. For those who attend Mass in the Extraordinary Form and follow the books in force in 1962, there is no problem. For those who attend the Ordinary Form, the Sunday meditations are no longer taken from the Sunday Mass readings. Reading from Divine Intimacy with that knowledge in hand, the meditations are still profitable, even more so to the person who also reads and meditates on the Mass readings of the day.

Fortunately, for those who incorporate reading from Divine Intimacy into their day, Chris Larmour provides the correct chapter each day under a international Creative Commons license at http://divineintimacy.larmour.us

Another obstacle to this practice is financial. Divine Intimacy is in print and available through Baronius Press, but the cost can be prohibitive for some. The leather-bound, gilt-edged edition is $60 before shipping. If enough people adopt this rule and regimen, of which Divine Intimacy is such an integral part, perhaps one of three things will happen. Baronius Press might release a cheaper, paperback version; a publishing arm of either O. Carm or O.C.D. will produce and distribute an affordable version; or someone will secure the rights to the text in order to distribute it electronically each day to subscribers. It is clear to me that one or all of these solutions is needed.

If you don't have access to the book, I can offer a few suggestions until you're able to secure a copy. First in order would be to find a copy of Fr. Thomas Dubay's "Fire Within" put out by Ignatius Press. It is a sure guide to the Carmelite path to contemplation through a thorough exposition of the writings of St. Catherine of Siena, St. John of the Cross, and St. Paul. Second would be to attempt on your own to prayerfully read through St. Catherine's "Interior Castle" or St. John of the Cross's "The Ascent of Mount Carmel" or "Dark Night of the Soul."

If for some reason you must choose your spiritual reading from sources outside of Carmel, there are too many good choices to list in full. From the Imitation of Christ to any of the Lives of the Saints, to de Montfort's True Devotion to Mary and beyond, the choices really are endless.

Often you will find, as you begin to implement this rule and regimen, that one practice bleeds into another, especially when related to the Wine Cellar. You may set aside a place within your home, or in quiet spaces outside your home, but the reality is that it is within you.

You will certainly, at times, be immersed in the sentiments expressed in Divine Intimacy and find yourself become silent before the Beloved, in contemplation of something true, good, or beautiful. The same is true of the daily readings and those contained within the Hours.

This is as it should be. It was designed to work that way. Do not shorten those moments unnecessarily, because they are the destination, the summit, the whole reason, the *unum necessarium* of Cellarium.

SUNDAY FELLOWSHIP

In Pope St. John Paul II's enyclical letter "Dies Domini" (The Lord's Day), the great pastor of souls lamented the replacement of the Lord's Day in recent days with the concept of "the weekend."

"Unfortunately, when Sunday loses its fundamental meaning and becomes merely part of a 'weekend,' (a weekly period of respite, spent perhaps far from home and often involving participation in cultural, political or sporting activities) it can happen that people stay locked within a horizon so limited that they can no longer see "the heavens." Hence, though ready to celebrate, they are really incapable of doing so[3].

He goes on to say that "disciples of Christ... are asked to avoid any confusion between the celebration of Sunday, which should truly be a way of keeping the Lord's Day holy, and the "weekend", understood as a time of simple rest and relaxation. This will require a genuine spiritual maturity, which will enable Christians to "be what they are", in full accordance with the gift of faith, always ready to give an account of the hope which is in them (cf. 1 Pt 3:15)."

While sports and other cultural activities will continue to dominate our "weekends" and consequently the Lord's Day, we

3   Dies Domini, 4

can approach it with spiritual maturity. Can these be part of a worthily celebrated Sabbath rest? They can if we keep the focus on the right things.

I've written in another book that man's greatest capacities are engaging in the celebration of beauty, truth, and goodness; wonder at the essence of everything in the world, the priority of love, the worship of God and pursuit of the highest things, of being subsumed in the immensity of all that is real, beyond the whispered beckoning of outward signs.

Sunday is leisure: celebration and festival. And so we must become the most celebratory and festive beings to ever have graced the face of the earth. Sunday is the Eighth Day. It is the Sabbath rest. And we should flock to our parishes and in gathering with our fellow parishioners each Sunday, to feast, celebrate, and enjoy fellowship with our brothers and sisters in the Faith.

A DAILY REGIMEN
"THE PEGS"

When we speak of a daily regimen, the first thing that distinguishes it from the rule of life is that it addresses those things we do at different times throughout the day. It can be as simple as resolving to pray as soon as we wake up and before going to bed, as well as saying grace before meals. It can include praying the Angelus at the traditional times, or praying the Divine Mercy chaplet at 3 p.m.

But if we look deeper at the history of the Church at prayer, along with the benefits of living in a hyper-connected world, it becomes obvious that our choices can give us more connection to the praying Church at large.

I'm talking about the Office, but I'm not referring to the popular television sitcom. I'm instead referring to the prayers that priests, monastics and other religious say each day under obedience, and which Vatican II recommended to all of the faithful.

Dealing as we are with a Carmelite spirituality, the choices available to us are the Liturgy of the Hours and the Little Office of the Blessed Virgin Mary. The Liturgy of the Hours was previously known as the *Officium Divinum* or the Divine Office and is still prayed as such by priests, religious, and laity attached to the Extraordinary Form of the liturgy.

The Little Office of the Blessed Virgin Mary is another matter. Though there are still some professed religious who pray it in common each day instead of the Divine Office or Liturgy of the Hours, it has in our day become something of a relic. And that is a shame, because it is worthy of our attention. In fact, it was closely tied to the requirements for obtaining the *Sabbatine Privilege*, and as such it has a deep connection to Carmel. When prayed individually as opposed to in community, it offers a shorter and more easily navigable text for those with other responsibilities. However, its structure still allows those who wish to gather together for prayer the means of adopting the attitudes and postures integral to its particular expression as communal prayer.

Whichever Hours you choose to base your Pegs on, or whatever other devotions you choose to practice at those times, the structure is basically the same. Let's get familiar with them:

First, the Offices are broken down into major and minor hours. The major hours are Matins (sounds like satins), Lauds (sounds like God's) and Vespers (sounds as one would expect). The minor hours are Prime (as expected), Terce (sounds like firs), Sext (sounds as expected), None (sounds like bone), and Compline (sounds like COM-plun).

The Invitatory (sounds as expected), while not one of the Hours, is a psalm with it's antiphon historically recited right before Matins. The traditional text is Psalm 95. In the Liturgy of the Hours, Psalm 24, 67 or 100 can be said in it's place. It is now said right before whichever Hour one begins the day with. That is normally The Office of Readings or Morning Prayer.

Matins was prayed at midnight, and was therefore known as a nocturnal hour. In the Liturgy of the Hours, it is now called the Office of Readings. and can be prayed at any time during the day or night.

Lauds was prayed at 3 a.m., being the second nocturnal hour, and in the Liturgy of the Hours is called Morning Prayer. In most places it is now prayed at around 6 a.m. instead of 3 a.m., the reason for which I'll explain in a moment.

The next few hours that follow Lauds take their names from the general time of day as reckoned from antiquity.

Prime means "first" as in the first hour of the day after the sun comes up. Terce means "third," Sext means "sixth" and None means "ninth" according to the same logic.

Prime was prayed at 6 a.m., and is suppressed in the LOTH. That is why it is most common now for Lauds to be prayed then.

Terce is prayed at around 9 a.m., and is known in the LOTH as Midmorning Prayer, part of Daytime Prayer.

Sext is prayed at around 12 p.m., and is known in the LOTH as Midday Prayer, part of Daytime Prayer.

None is prayed at around 3 p.m., and is known in the LOTH as Midafternoon Prayer, part of Daytime Prayer.

Vespers is prayed at around 6 p.m., and is known in the LOTH as Evening Prayer.

Compline is prayed before going to bed, and is known in the LOTH as Night Prayer.

Probably the greatest benefit of adopting this framework is that the Psalms around which they are composed teach us how to pray. There is not an emotion or sentiment experienced daily in a Christian's life that is not addressed. From exstatic joy to wailing grief, from the depths of divine love to the sorrows of all that life on earth entails, the Psalms take them up as their subjects.

The subjects are rich for meditation and contemplation. Many of the psalms are prophetic, speaking of Our Lord in intimate detail. Their advice is full of wisdom. Their imagery is palpable. Like the rest of sacred scripture, they afford anyone willing to invest the time to pray them the opportunity to allow the Word of the Lord to wash over them and renew their his mind in the Holy Spirit.

And so this is the framework that the Cellarium regimen adopts for driving the Pegs into your calendar each day with periodic reminders to return to the Source, to God, with whatever gifts or burdens you bear in your hands, with whatever sentiments or worries occupy your mind.

As a foretaste of what is to come if you simply begin your regimen with praying the *Nunc Dimmitis* and it's antiphon each day before going to sleep, consider the beautiful imagery of keeping watch with Christ. With every Night Prayer in the Liturgy of the Hours, bracketing the Nunc Dimmitis, we recite this petition:

"Protect us, Lord, as we stay awake; watch over us as we sleep, that awake we may keep watch with Christ, and asleep, rest in his peace."

It is followed by Simeon's short prophecy at the presentation of Our Lord in the Temple, and then the antiphon is again repeated.

"Lord, now you let your servant go in peace; your word has been fulfilled. My own eyes have seen the salvation which you have prepared in the sight of every people: a light to reveal you to the nations and the glory of your people Israel."

The petition is misunderstood by some to encompass the whole day. But the language suggests otherwise. Before we were enslaved by alarm clocks, days were governed by the rhythms of nature, and of the rising and setting of the sun, along with a little help from parish church bells! Summer nights are shorter, and winter nights much longer. Those entrusted with watching over the city broke the night into watches, or shifts. Nobody was expected to keep watch through the whole night, but our God never sleeps, and so he watches over us through the entire night.

So even at night, we are asked to accompany the Lord in "watching over the city." Especially during those long winter nights, families would normally go to bed shortly after the sun set and spend their nights in successive waking and sleeping cycles.

While awake, families would take part in quiet conversations and prayers until sleep visited again. This went on until the landscape stirred with the breaking of dawn. It is in this context that we pray "protect us, Lord, as we stay awake." It is during the waking hours or watches of the night, not the day. "Watch over us as we sleep." For sleep we must. "That awake we may keep watch with Christ." Our hearts joined with His in attentive care. "And asleep, rest in His peace." A peace which passes all understanding.

If you make this prayer your own before retiring for the day, you will not only be fulfilling your duty toward God, you will be praying with the whole Church spread throughout the world as the sunlight leaves the sky in it's course.

The Pegs - A Daily Regimen

The daily regimen creates space at these set hours each day where you pause to recognize the presence of God and give him the time and attention, the praise and worship which He is due.

In the following chapter, I'll show you how to begin implementing the rule and regimen so that you can ease into it with the with only a little effort, while gradually acquiring the habits that will point you firmly in the direction of the Saints.

How to Use the Planner

Daily Regimen

The engine that drives the Cellarium rule and regimen is the Weekly Preview. Especially in the beginning, you'll want to take stock of your current schedule, your commitments, and all of the details of your life each day and see where you can begin plugging the Pegs into your calendar.

Based on that, it makes the most sense to begin with the regimen. As we discussed earlier, the framework is taken from the Hours (Liturgy of the Hours or "The Hours of Our Lady" as the Little Office of the Blessed Virgin Mary is sometimes called.

Step one is to use the technology available to you, to create the daily appointments with alarms that will remind you to place yourself in the presence of God and to pray whatever devo-

Calendar - The Pegs

Mother and Lauds

6

Prime

7

8

9

Terce

10

11

12

Sext

1

2

3

None

4

5

6

Vespers

7

8

Compline

tion you decided upon for that week. While I found it helpful to create the appointments all at once, whether or not I was going to hang a devotion to that particular peg for the week, you are certainly not bound to do that. It was helpful for me to get used to the alarms going off throughout the day, with the knowledge that I would one day be putting more weight on those Pegs. It is easy, with each reminder, to simply stop what I'm doing for a moment, recognize His presence, and if nothing else simply say "Jesus, I love you. Help me to love you more and more."

The hours you choose for the reminders to go off is obviously up to you. They are generally prayed "in the vicinity of" the time they're scheduled each day. How early one wants Lauds to chime, or how late to set Compline for, is up to each individual. The important thing is to set them!

To start this practice, especially if you don't have access yet to the Liturgy of the Hours, Divine Office, of the Little Office, it is perfectly fine to stop and pray any prayer. You're forming the habit, and that is what matters most. Once you decide which form of the Office you want to use, it is time to secure a copy. Fortunately there are a range of choices, from free apps to more or less expensive paper editions.

iBreviary app

Apps for the Liturgy of the Hours include iBreviary and Divine Office. I've included screen shots of them here to you'll know you've got the right ones when you look for them in your mobile device's app store. I don't have a preference between the two since I'm more of a tactile person and normally use paper devotional books. I do like that the Divinie Office app includes audio files for each hour, so if you're ever stuck in traffic or another place where you can't read from a book,

Divine Office app

they've got you covered. Print versions of the Liturgy of the Hours are available from Catholic Book Publishing as the St. Joseph Liturgy of the Hours four-volume set in hardback, black leather with gilt pages, or in a cheaper imitation leather set.

Since the LOTH is built around the four-week psalm cycle, CBP makes available two shorter versions of the LOTH. There is the one-volume Christian Prayer, and for bare minimalists, the thin but mighty Shorter Christian Prayer which contains only the four-week psalter for Morning and Evening Prayer.

For those attached to the Extraordinary Form and the liturgical books in force in 1962, you are lucky that Baronius Press has released a magnificent three-volume set of the Roman Breviary in black leather binding. You are unfortunate in that it costs $380. That's definitely something to have everyone chip in on as a Christmas gift.

For the economically disadvantaged (and the just plain *cheapos* among us), the same words are available *sans papier* over at divinumofficium.com. Don't try to type that in, just scan this QR code and it'll take you there.

This version gives you the option to pray several different historical versions of the Office. From the 1570 version from the Council of Trent, to the 1960 including the New Calendar, you have the opportunity to delve in and see how it has changed throughout history (and in the end, see that it really hasn't changed much). There is  also the ability to compare two versions, including the Office for the Dead (Defunctorum) and the Little Office of the Blessed Virgin Mary (Parvum B.M.V).

And speaking of Our Lady, if you choose to use the Little Office of the Blessed Virgin Mary to set the prayer structure of your day, you have several options. Once again Baronius Press has a solid offering in the LOBVM with included Gregorian chant, bound in blue leather for a reasonable $30.

Free versions, most notably the one from the above mentioned divinumofficium.com (scan the QR), as well as lower priced copies, abound on Amazon and from other online book-sellers. If you are interested in an English only version with music included for the hymns and detailed rubrics interspersed with the text, the only one in existance is "The Hours of Our Lady" which is unfortunately published by the author of this book. I published it because it didn't exist, it needed to exist, and for those who ever wish to pray the Little Office in common, and get the details right, it's the only guide available that trains you as you go.

Once you have set your reminders to go off, and have gotten to the point where you're ready to begin praying the Hours, I recommend that you begin with one or two, such as Lauds and Vespers, and even then to begin with perhaps one psalm and it's antiphon, or the Canticle of Zechariah for Lauds or the Magnificat at Vespers.

Choose what you will add to the Pegs for the coming week, and write it into "The Pegs" section of your Weekly Preview. From there you will transfer the information onto the calendar in the daily planner pages for the upcoming week, over top of the light gray Hours to the right of the pegs. Your first week might say "the first Psalm and Antiphon" over top of Vespers. That's great. Do it each day that week.

As you progress deeper into prayer, you will know intuitively what you can do or cannot pray at each hour. You can pack a lot of piety into the reading of a single Psalm. You can simply recognize the presence of God at the other hours, and whisper a

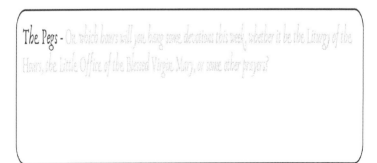

The Pegs - On which hours will you hang some devotions this week, whether it be the Liturgy of the Hours, the Little Office of the Blessed Virgin Mary, or some other prayers?

heartfelt, loving glance at the others.

RULE OF LIFE

Most of the practices listed under the rule are things that reach beyond your calendar. You will strive to the best of your ability to maintain them as constants each day. Of course, none of us are perfect, so there will be times when you fall far from the ideal. It's part of being human. But as they are tied to the virtues, you will find over time that as your prayer life deepens, you will increase in virtue, and in some instances natural (and hard won) virtues will be overtaken by infused, supernatural virtue. A few of the practices transcend categories, or could be listed under both. A couple of examples are descending into the Wine Cellar, praying the Rosary, and daily Mass when it is possible for you to attend. They're part of the rule because they don't strictly follow the structure of the Hours, and opportunities may arise for you to do them as time allows. What is most important, however, is that you begin to live them.

THE BROWN SCAPULAR

Seeking enrollment in and constantly wearing the brown scapular of Our Lady of Mount Carmel is an integral step in adopting the Cellarium rule of life. It is the habit of Carmel. Through it we share in the spiritual benefits of the order. The Church has long defended the use of this scapular as a constant testimony that we belong to Mary. It is her assurance of her protection. It is our constant reminder to imitate her. The rite of enrollment can be found in the back matter of this planner, and scheduling it should be as easy as contacting your parish rectory and discussing it with a priest. Any Catholic priest with faculties can do it for you. If you are of a certain age, and don't remember all the details of your First Communion, ask around as to whether you were enrolled at that time. It was a common practice for many years.

If it takes some time before you are able to be enrolled, don't worry. You can wear the scapular beforehand, and I would highly recommend it. If you have a Catholic supply store near you, they will most likely have brown scapulars there. If not, there are dozens of merchants online that make and sell them.

CHASTITY

These are difficult times in which to live a life of purity. We're assaulted every day from every side with vices which in better times were hidden. What I will say here is to reiterate that if you struggle for purity, and are looking for real, tangible assistance, you need look no further than to your brown scapular. The protection promised by Mary includes her intervention, her intercession, her very mantle spread over you like a shield that deflects the enemy's firey darts.

THE WINE CELLAR

This is one of the elements of the rule of life that transcends the calendar and other categories. Everything else in the rule and regimen are secondary to it. If you take no other practice away from reading this book, make it this one. I cannot stress this enough. Whiile in a very real sense, we owe to God in justice at least fifteen minutes per day of silent prayer, even that will be difficult for some because of the demands of their schedule or because of poor use of time. These things take time to correct, but the answer is to begin somewhere. you will be distracted. You will find it hard to focus. And it may seem for a long time that nothing special is happening. But it will be happening, because you're showing up and shutting up, and responding to Our Lord's call to reciprocate His love.

We are constantly bombarded with noise, and it makes it all the more difficult to focus on God, because God dwells in silence, and we must approach him daily in silence. If you'd like to read further on the subject, I would recommend Cardinal Sarah's "The Power of Silence." But outside of the practice of scheduling time each day "in the wine cellar" you will often find yourself recollected and closer to God, particularly after praying the Psalms or meditating on the day's passage from Fr. Gabriel's "Divine Intimacy." While you probably won't write those times

Wine Cellar - How long will you spend each day in silent contemplation?

into the Wine Cellar entry in your Weekly Preview, I encourage you to comment on it in the "Last Week's Review" section each Sunday when you're reflecting on it, and preparing for the upcoming week. And do your best on being generous in filling in the Wine Cellar entry in the Weekly Preview. If you know that you'll be setting time aside at the same hour each day, go ahead and put it on your daily calendar.

THE ROSARY AND INTERCESSION

As a beginner, it may be intimidating to think about praying the Rosary each day, but that sentiment will soon be dashed once you begin, at whatever level you are able each day, to answer Our Lady's plea. As with each of the other areas in the rule of life, you'll start with what you are able to manage, understanding that you are under no strict obligations. This is all voluntary on your part. If your entry point for praying the Rosary each day is a single decade of one mystery, start there, and schedule it into your Weekly Preview. You'll notice that I tied the Rosary and Intercession together into one entry. There is a reason for that. As stated earlier, we should always pray the Rosary for specific intentions, and reciting some part of the Rosary each day is our way of fulfilling that obligation to pray for others. The chief obligation in the spiritual works of mercy is to pray for the living and the dead. I encourage you to create a master prayer list somewhere you'll be able to access it from anywhere, and to begin populating it with names and intentions.

The daily and weekly transferring of prayer intentions is intentional in Cellarium. It brings those people and intentions to mind each time you do it. Build the habit, but start from where you are. Write down the names you can think of, from people

Rosary and Intercession. - *How many decades will you pray each day for the Intercession of those on your prayer list?*

who have asked you to pray for them, and those for whom you should be praying without them having to ask. As your list grows, make time each week to prayerfully read through the whole list, preferably on Sunday when you're reviewing the previous week and planning for the next.

CONSPICUOUS SILENCE

As stated earlier in the instruction, observing silence and keeping watch over our tongues is not optional for a disciple of Christ. Beginning in earnest to live it can be an eye-opening experience because it is difficult, especially in these times. We're constantly bombarded with noise and distractions everywhere we go. It is a good habit to pause before speaking to ask ourselves if what we're about to say is necessary, if we are the ones that should be saying it, and whether it is helpful, true, or spoken with humility and love.

Doing this forces us to be recollected each time we remember to practice it. And believe me, as fallen creatures, we won't always remember to do it, and will often regret what we've said after we say it. But we can learn from our mistakes and stop to ask forgiveness from God for the times when we didn't live up to the rule. It is a good thing to go back and ask forgiveness from those we may have offended.

Carmelites who have taken a vow of silence normally exercise it strictly from after Vespers until Lauds. That roughly correlates to the hours we are asleep with a bit of time in the evening, and while the our state in life may require conversation during that time, we should still remind ourselves to stick to what is true, helpful, and necessary.

FASTING AND FEASTING

Having already discussed in some depth the Church's laws on

fasting and abstinence, as well as the traditional times that Carmelites practice fasting and abstaining from meat, what remains is for you to decide where you will begin, and make the entry into your Weekly Preview.

A logical entry point is simply to obey the Church's immemorial practice of abstaining from meat on all Fridays of the year, even outside of Lent, because that was always her intent, even

Silence - How will you practice interior recollection this week?

after the pain of sin was removed from contradiction of the practice. Writing it down and tracking it each week will help you to keep it in mind, and will lessen the chance that you'll forget. If you do forget, just move on and resolve to do better next time. On other days, it is your choice whether you simply fast or abstain, but make sure that what you schedule is achievable. Of course, the Church's calendar is replete with solemnities, feasts, memorials, and optional memorials. Those days often supercede the requirement to fast or abstain. Our human need to celebrate, to be at leisure, and to participate in festivities was placed there by God. Of course we can deny ourselves for the love of God, or even for vain reasons, but self-denial is the denial of things that are naturally good, perhaps even good for us.

That is why Sunday is always a feast day, a weekly Easter. Once you begin to take fasting and abstinence seriously and practice it weekly, you will get into a rhythm. I won't say it's something you'll ever relish, but keeping close track of the week's upcoming feast days and days of fasting and abstinence will prime the pump, in a sense, and prepare you for what is to come. When you're feasting, feast. Not to the point of gluttony, of course. And when you're fasting and abstaining, strive to do it well. Go lightly when you first start, and build up a firm habitual base.

GOSPEL POVERTY

If there is one element to the rule that will generate the most kickback, my guess will be that it's in regard to the absolute Gospel mandate that a disciple of Jesus Christ practice material poverty. It seems like folly. It runs counter to everything in the modern world. And yet, it is right there in black and white whenever Christ addresses what we must do if we want to follow Hiim. We must renounce everything and take up our cross if we wish to follow Him. He made no exception.

That doesn't mean you can't have an honest, good paying job, it means you are to live sparingly and give the poor and downtrodden what is due to them in justice. It doesn't mean you can't wear nice clothes if your state in life demands it, it means that you should have the mind of a St. Thomas More, who wore rough, scratchy, penitential undergarments beneath the finery required of his office.

Practically speaking, it means that if you have two coats, you give one of them away, and if your life is ruled by the things you own, you start paring down, minimizing, and simplifying. How you do that each week is such a personal matter that it's best left up to each individual in his or her circumstances, but as an entry into your Weekly Preview, I suggest coming up with something substantial each week, and doing your best to make it happen.

DIVINE INTIMACY

Continuing the thought from Spiritual Formation section in

the chapter A Rule of Life above, I cannot stress enough how strongly I recommend that you obtain a copy of Fr. Gabriel's book Divine Intimacy, and allow it to form you in the spirit and thought of Carmel. Remember that Chris Larmour has identified the appropriate reading for each day at http://divineintimacy.larmour.us

Deciding on the Weekly Preview which parts you will read each week will guide you through the topics over the course of a

Sparing and Sharing - What measures will you take this week to give God control of what he has blessed you with?

year. Part catechism, part spiritual direction, and part meditation, it will often lead you to contemplation as you conform yourself to it's teachings. As a practical matter, placing the appropriate chapter number on your daily spread is as easy as transferring them from Mr. Larmour's list. This is your continuing Carmelite formation and yet so much more. Until you are able to secure a copy of Divine Intimacy, consider my advice for other works to fill it's place, many of which can be purchased at minimal cost, but for the long run, I consider there to be no reasonable replacement if you wish to make full progress through the Cellarium rule and regimen.

DAILY MASS/MASS READINGS

As helpful as it is to meditate on the daily Mass readings, which allow the Scriptures to wash over our lives, it is even more helpful for us to pursue the graces both natural and supernatural which flow from attending Holy Mass as often as we are able. Our state in life will obviously dictate how often that can be, but the willingness to do so will open doors in our souls and give us the opportunity to unite ourselves to Christ in the Blessed Sacrament and to join our prayer intentions to the sacrifice offered each day on the altars within our reach. It is the same sacrifice offered around the world, and the more often we unite ourselves, the more opportunities we have to grow in holiness.

Even if it is not possible to be at a church or cathedral at the times when Mass is celebrated, it is often still possible to stop by a church for a few moments of Eucharistic adoration. Our Lord craves our presence, and waits for us, willingly captive in the tabernacle. In the absence of our availability to go in person, we must form the daily habit of reading the Mass texts of the day, meditating on them, incorporating them into our lives, and making a spiritual Communion. The graces that flow from this easily attainable practice are unimagineable.

When you've worked out whether or not you'll be able to attend one or more daily Masses, or will read the texts of the day, whether in full or in part, mark them on your Weekly Preview. Even if you meditate on the Collect prayer of the Gospel, it will enrich your spiritual life.

Sunday Fellowship

Sunday fellowship makes place and time for the actualization of what we discussed earlier under the heading of Spiritual Formation. I've said before that Catholicism is a team sport. We live in flesh and it is part of our nature to form bonds with others. We are conjugal creatures. We need friendships and relationships with family to fully live as human beings. God created us for others, as gifts. Spiritual friendships especially are central to our ability to remain well-adjusted and social creatures.

It is also in our deepest nature to celebrate. Our need for festivity (which the Church has always understood) and the leisure to focus on the higher things is has largely been ripped from us today and has been replaced with cheap trinkets in the exchange. Worship is the highest form of festivity and celebration known to fallen man, and the Mass is the highest form of worship.

I could wish that a serious re-evaluation of our current treatment of Sunday as part of what JPII called "the weekend" would take place among Catholics, and that they would make a mature decision to reject it in favor of day-long celebrations of the Lord's Day - a day devoted to Mass but also to fellowship with our brothers and sisters in whatever legitimate forms it might take.

Finding others willing to do much of anything beyond going to a restaurant for a nice meal after Mass could prove difficult if more people don't start to take it seriously, but even shopping or dining out on the Lord's Day can be problematic if done with full knowledge of the law being transgressed. That transgression is a breach of solidarity against others who are forced to work on a day on which they should be at leisure to also pursue the highest things.

PRINTING AND USING THE PLANNER

If you have access to a photocopier, it's possible to simply print the planner pages, front and back. The first two are the Weekly Preview and prayer list, and the second two are the Daily Pages with cover and room on the back for reflections. Printer settings should be double sided, print on short edge.

The pages are also available as free, full page PDF downloads at:

https://bit.ly/3hUphbw

Also available from jimgarlits.com in the following formats:

QUARTERLY 2-PAGE PER DAY PAPER PLANNER
FULL YEAR DIGITAL DAILY PLANNER

Weekly Preview
Month Day - Day

Last Week's Review - What went well and what do you need to work on?

Scapular - Wear it daily and wash it today!

Wine Cellar - How long will you spend each day in silent contemplation?

Rosary and Intercession - How many decades will you pray each day for the intercession of those on your prayer list?

Silence - How will you practice interior recollection this week?

Fasting and Abstinence - On which days and in what ways will you fast or abstain from meat this week?

Sparing and Sharing - What measures will you take this week to give God control of what he has blessed you with?

Chastity - What will you do this week to guard your senses for the sake of purity?

Divine Intimacy - Which sections will you read each day this week, or what will you read in it's place?
Presence of God   First   Meditation   Second   Meditation   Colloquy

Daily Mass - On which days will you attend daily Mass this week?

Mass Readings
Su Mo Tu We Th Fr Sa
Introit   Collect   First Reading
Responsorial Psalm   Gospel

The Pegs - On which hours will you hang some devotions this week, whether it be the Liturgy of the Hours, the Little Office of the Blessed Virgin Mary, or some other prayers?

Sunday Fellowship - With whom will you gather outside of Mass this Sunday to strengthen the bonds of love and solidarity?

URGENT REQUESTS

AMILY

ARISH

WEEKLY INTERCESSIONS

FRIENDS

WORK

SOCIAL MEDIA

Reflections:

the
Cellarium
Daily Planner
Page

Month / *Day* / *Year*

BASED ON THE RULE AND REGIMEN
for the
BROWN SCAPULAR CONFRATERNITY
of
OUR LADY OF MOUNT CARMEL

Weekday/ Month/Day

Rosary: Mystery
Liturgical Season
Saint's Feast or Memorial
Divine Intimacy Chapter

What passage most moved you from your readings today?

Tasks - Do everything for the glory of God

1
2
3

Matins and Lauds

6
Prime

7

8

9
Terce

10

11

12
Sext

1

2

3
None

4

5

6
Vespers

7

8

Compline

√ = Done   / = Deferred   O = Delegated   X = Deleted

The Regs - Cellarium
Rule of Life

) Wear the Brown Scapular
) Descend into the Wine Cellar
) Pray the Rosary
) Intercession
) Conspicuous Silence
) Gospel Poverty
) Chastity
) Fasting and Abstinence
) Mass/Daily Mass Readings
) Spiritual Reading/Divine Intimacy
) Sunday Fellowship

Transfer these to the Intercession section at the end of the day

Notes

☐ = Do   O = Delegate   ! = Important   ? = Question

Rite for the Blessing of and Enrollment in the Scapular of the Blessed Virgin Mary of Mount Carmel

Preliminaries

1. The blessing of, and enrollment in, the Scapular of the Blessed Virgin Mary of Mount Carmel should preferably take place within a community celebration.

2. The enrollment of the Scapular implies affiliation to the Carmelite Family. Priests and deacons have the faculties for blessing Scapulars; other authorized persons may enroll the faithful.

3. The traditional form of the Scapular must be used for the blessing and enrollment. It may then be replaced by the appropriate medal.

4. The blessing of and enrollment in the Scapular takes place according to the rites and prayers hereunder. The usual form includes the opening rite, a reading of the Word of God and the intercessions, the prayer of blessing and the enrollment in the scapular the closing rite. In this manner the meaning of the Scapular in the lives of the faithful who receive it is fully conveyed.

5. It is necessary that in both formulas, the spiritual meaning of the graces attached to the Scapular of our Lady of Mount Carmel be expressed, as also the obligations assumed through this sign of devotion to the holy Virgin.

Opening rite

6. The officiant welcomes the faithful gathered before the main altar or before a picture of our Lady.

Opening hymn or a moment of silence.

Min. In the name of the Father, and of the Son and of the Holy Spirit.

R/. Amen.

Min. The Lord be with you.

R/. And also with you.

7. The officiant invites those present to take part in the rite of blessing of and enrollment in the Scapular with the following or other similar words, which explain the nature of this celebration:

When Jesus walked on earth, whoever even touched the hem of his garment became whole. We praise the Lord, because in his

Church he continues to use the humblest of means to show us his infinite mercy. We too can use these means to glorify the Lord, to express our desire to serve him and to renew our life-long commitment of fidelity made at our baptism.

This Scapular of our Lady of Mount Carmel is a sign of the motherly love of the Virgin Mary, which reminds us of her care for the members of the Carmelite family, especially in moments of great need. It is a love which invites love in return.

This Scapular is a sign of communion with the Order of the Brothers of the Blessed Virgin Mary of Mount Carmel dedicated to the service of our Lady for the good of the whole Church. With this Scapular you express the desire to take part in the spirit and life of the Order.

The Scapular is a mirror of the humility and purity of Mary: through her simplicity she invites us to live modestly and in purity. By wearing the Scapular day and night, it becomes a sign of our constant prayer and of our special dedication to the love and service of the Virgin Mary.

By wearing the Scapular, you renew your baptismal vow to put on our Lord Jesus Christ. In Mary, your hope of salvation will be safeguarded, because in her the God of Life has made his abode.

THE WORD OF GOD

8. One of those present reads a text from Sacred Scripture. The texts quoted below refer particularly to the mystery of salvation or to devotion to the holy Virgin. One of the following texts may be chosen: a) From the Old Testament

Pr 8: 17-21. I love those who love me.

Is 61: 1-2, 10. He has clothed me with a mantle of justice.

2 K 2: 7-13. The mantle of Elijah fell on Elisha.

Ba 5: 1-5. Clothe yourselves with the beauty of God.

Ezk 16: 8-14. Your beauty was perfect.

b) From the New Testament

Rm 12: 1-2. This is your spiritual worship.

Ga 4: 4-7. God sent his Son born of a woman.

Ep 6: 10-17. Take strength from the Lord.

Mk 5: 25-34. The woman touched the garment of Jesus and was cured.

Lk 2: 4-8. Mary wrapped her Firstborn in swaddling clothes.

9. A short exhortation.

Brown Scapular Enrollment

After the reading, the officiant addresses those present briefly to explain, in the light of the Word of God, the meaning of the celebration, the graces and obligations attached to the Scapular.

INTERCESSIONS

10. There follows the prayers of intercession. At this point a few intentions are prayed for. The most suitable prayers may be chosen or other prayers which are more suitable for the occasion may be added. The officiant invites all to pray:

Min. Dear sisters and brothers, we enjoy the patronage of the Virgin Mary, Mother of God. In her womb the Word of God put on our mortality by taking on our flesh. Let us pray the Father that, by the power of the Holy Spirit, we may reflect Jesus, our brother, in our lives, and so let us say:

R/. Lord, grant that we may be clothed in Jesus Christ.

Holy Father, who clothed your Son with our human flesh in order that we might participate in the divine life, — grant that, by the intercession of the Virgin Mary, his perfect disciple, we may be clothed in his divinity.

Holy Father, who wished that your Son may become like us in all things but sin, so that, by the following in his footsteps, we might conform to his image in all things, — grant that, by the intercession of the Virgin Mary, we may imitate Christ and be pleasing to you in all our works.

Holy Father, who invites us to the banquet of grace, clothed in bridal attire in order to reveal your love for us, — by the intercession of the Virgin Mary, clothe us with her active charity and her loving service.

Holy Father, who have clothed Mary with the sun, and through her have crushed the head of the serpent, — by the intercession of the Virgin, grant that we may be able to overcome the snares of the evil one in our life and in the world we live in.

Holy Father, who chose Mary to be the daughter of the New Testament, — by the intercession of Mary, Virgin of the New Heart, purify our hearts and strengthen our faith.

Holy Father, who have looked upon the lowliness of your Handmaid, and through her lips have proclaimed the strength of your arm, — by the intercession of Mary, grant that we may be prophets of your Kingdom, that we may proclaim your mercy to every generation.

Holy Father, you gave your Son a mother who wrapped him in swaddling clothes, — by the intercession of the Virgin Mother, grant that we may love the poor and the marginalized, and that we may be united to them in building a world which is more just and fraternal.

Holy Father, who have wrapped us with the mantle of justice and holiness, — by the intercession of the Virgin Mary, sanctify us in Christ and make us generous collaborators in the work of the salvation of this world.

Holy Father, who have blessed us with every spiritual blessing in Christ, — by the intercession of the Virgin Mary, grant that we may happily pass from death to life.

PRAYER OF THE BLESSING

11. The priest or deacon, with arms outstretched, says this prayer of blessing.

Min. O God, author and perfection of holiness, who call those who were born of water and the Holy Spirit to the fullness of the Christian life, look with kindness on those who are about to receive devoutly the Scapular of Carmel which they will wear faithfully as the sign of their commitment to the Virgin Mary of Mount Carmel. Grant that in surrendering to the love of the most tender Virgin, they may conform themselves to the image of Jesus Christ your Son, and having run the course of this life happily, may they enter into the joy of your house. Through Christ our Lord.

R/. Amen

The priest or deacon then sprinkles holy water.

ENROLLMENT IN THE SCAPULAR

12. The officiant then places the Scapular on each faithful who has requested it, and says:

Receive this Scapular. (Through this Scapular you become a member of the Confraternity of the Blessed Virgin Mary of Mount Carmel.) Full of faith in the love of such a great Mother, dedicate yourself to imitating her and to a special relationship with her. Wear this sign as a reminder of the presence of Mary in your daily commitment to be clothed in Jesus Christ and to manifest him in your life for the good of the Church and the whole of humanity, and to the glory of the Most Blessed Trinity.

R/. Amen.

13. If deemed more appropriate, when there are many persons

to be enrolled in the Scapular, the officiant may say the form of enrollment once only. Then all together answer Amen and approach the officiant to receive the Scapular.

14. After enrollment, the officiant addresses all in these words:

Having received the Scapular, you have been received into the family of Carmel, consecrated in a special way to the imitation and service of the Virgin Mother of God, that you may live for Christ and his Church in the contemplative and apostolic spirit of the Order of Carmel. And that you may be able to follow this ideal perfectly, by the faculties entrusted to me, I admit you to participate in all the spiritual benefits of the Order of Carmel.

15. After explaining briefly and clearly the commitment and obligations involved in being admitted institutionally to the Carmelite family, the officiant closes the rite with a solemn blessing.

Closing rite

16. The priest or deacon stretches his hands over those present.

Min. May the Father pour on you his merciful love given to us in Christ Jesus, son of the Virgin Mary.

R/. Amen.

Min. May Jesus Christ grant you to partake of the love of the Father in the motherly warmth of the Virgin of Carmel, that you become doers of every good.

R/. Amen.

Min. The Holy Spirit has inspired you to place yourselves under the mantle of Mary, may he make you apostles in the way of justice and peace.

R/. Amen.

Min. And may the blessing of almighty God, the Father, and the Son and the Holy Spirit descend upon you and remain with your forever.

R/. Amen.

17. The celebration may end with an appropriate hymn to Our Lady, for instance, Flos Carmeli, Salve Regina, Sub tuum praesidium.